JEN WILKIN

1 PETER

A LIVING HOPE IN CHRIST

TGC THE GOSPEL COALITION
WOMEN'S INITIATIVES

LifeWay Press®
Nashville, Tennessee

Published by LifeWay Press® • © 2015 Jen Wilkin

ISBN: 9781430051541

Item: 005772639

Dewey Decimal Classification: 227.92
Subject Headings: BIBLE. N.T. 1 PETER--STUDY AND TEACHING / CHRISTIAN LIFE / INTERPERSONAL RELATIONS

All Scripture quotations, unless otherwise noted, are taken from The Holy Bible, English Standard Version® (ESV®), copyright © 2001 by Crossway, a publishing ministry of Good News Publishers. Used by permission. All rights reserved. Scripture quotations marked NIV are taken from The Holy Bible, NEW INTERNATIONAL VERSION®, Copyright © 1973, 1978, 1984, 2011 by Biblica, Inc. All rights reserved worldwide. Used by permission.

To order additional copies of this resource, order online at www.lifeway.com; write LifeWay Christian Resources Customer Service: One LifeWay Plaza, Nashville, TN 37234-0113; fax order to 615.251.5933; or call toll-free 1.800.458.2772.

Printed in the United States of America

Adult Ministry Publishing
LifeWay Resources
One LifeWay Plaza
Nashville, TN 37234-0152

PRODUCTION TEAM

AUTHOR:
JEN WILKIN

EDITORIAL MANAGER:
AMY LOWE

ART DIRECTOR:
HEATHER WETHERINGTON

CONTENT EDITOR:
ELIZABETH HYNDMAN

PRODUCTION EDITOR:
ANGELA REED

DIRECTOR, LIFEWAY
ADULT MINISTRY:
FAITH WHATLEY

EDITORIAL PROJECT
LEADER:
MICHELLE HICKS

VIDEO PRODUCER &
DIRECTOR:
TIM COX

CONTENTS

HOW SHOULD WE APPROACH GOD'S WORD?

OUR PURPOSE

The Bible study you are about to begin may be different than studies you have done in the past. It will not cover a specific topic from all angles. It will not have poetry or stories that leave you laughing, crying, or inspired. It will not focus on answering the question, "What does the Bible say about me?" It will not aid you in self-discovery, at least not as its primary intent.

What it will do is teach you an important passage of the Bible in a way that will stay with you for years to come. It will challenge you to move beyond loving God with just your heart to loving Him with your mind. It will focus on answering the question, "What does the Bible say about God?" It will aid you in the worthy task of God-discovery.

You see, the Bible is not a book about self-discovery; it is a book about God-discovery. The Bible is God's declared intent to make Himself known to us. In learning about the character of God in Scripture we will experience self-discovery, but it must not be the focus of our study. The focus must be God Himself.

This focus changes the way we study. We look first for what a passage can teach us about the character of God, allowing self-discovery to be the byproduct of God-discovery. This is a much better approach because there can be no true knowledge of self apart from knowledge of God. So when I read the account of Jonah, I see first that God is just and faithful to His Word—He is faithful to proclaim His message to Nineveh no matter what. I see second that I, by contrast (and much like Jonah), am unjust to my fellow man and unfaithful to God's Word. Thus, knowledge of God leads to true knowledge of self, which leads to repentance and transformation. This is what Paul meant when he wrote that we are transformed by the renewing of our minds (Rom. 12:2).

Women are good at loving God with their hearts. We are good at engaging our emotions in our pursuit of God. But the God who commands us to love with the totality of our heart, soul, and strength also commands us to love Him with all of our minds. Because He only commands what He also enables His children to do, it must be possible for us to love Him well with our minds or He would not command it. I know you will bring your emotions to your study of God's Word, and that is good and right. But it is your mind that I want to engage. God intends for you to be a good student, renewing your mind and thus transforming your heart.

OUR PROCESS

Being a good student entails following good study habits. When we sit down to read, most of us like to read through a particular passage and then find a way to apply it to our everyday lives. We may read through an entire book of the Bible over a period of time, or we may jump around from place to place. I want to suggest a different approach, one that may not always yield immediate application, comfort, or peace, but one that builds over time a cumulative understanding of the message of Scripture.

READING IN CONTEXT AND REPETITIVELY

Imagine yourself receiving a letter in the mail. The envelope is hand-written, but you don't glance at the return address. Instead you tear open the envelope, flip to the second page, read two paragraphs near the bottom, and set the letter aside. Knowing that if someone bothered to send it to you, that you should act on its contents in some way, you spend a few minutes trying to figure out how to respond to what the section you just read had to say. What are the odds you will be successful?

No one would read a letter this way. But this is precisely the way many of us read our Bibles. We skip past reading the "envelope"—Who wrote this? To whom is it written? When was it written? Where was it written?—and then try to determine the purpose of its contents from a portion of the whole. What if we took time to read the envelope? What if, after determining the context for its writing, we started at the beginning and read to the end? Wouldn't that make infinitely more sense?

In our study we will take this approach to Scripture. We will begin by placing our text in its historical and cultural context. We will "read the envelope." Then we will read through the entire text multiple times, so that we can better determine what it wants to say to us. We will read repetitively so that we might move through three critical stages of understanding: comprehension, interpretation, and application.

STAGE 1: COMPREHENSION

Remember the reading comprehension section on the SAT? Remember those long reading passages followed by questions to test your knowledge of what you had just read? The objective was to force you to read for detail. We are going to apply the same method to our study of God's Word. When we read for comprehension we ask ourselves, "What does it say?" This is hard work. A person who comprehends the account of the six days of creation can tell you specifically what happened on each day. This is the first step toward being able to interpret and apply the story of creation to our lives.

STAGE 2: INTERPRETATION

While comprehension asks, "What does it say?," interpretation asks, "What does it mean?" Once we have read a passage enough times to know what it says, we are ready to look into its meaning. A person who interprets the creation story can tell you why God created in a particular order or way. She is able to imply things from the text beyond what it says.

STAGE 3: APPLICATION

After doing the work to understand what the text says and what the text means, we are finally ready to ask, "How should it change me?" Here is where we draw on our God-centered perspective to ask three supporting questions:

- What does this passage teach me about God?

- How does this aspect of God's character change my view of self?

- What should I do in response?

A person who applies the creation story can tell us that because God creates in an orderly fashion, we too should live well-ordered lives. Knowledge of God gleaned through comprehension of the text and interpretation of its meaning can now be applied to my life in a way that challenges me to be different.

SOME GUIDELINES

It is vital to the learning process that you allow yourself to move through the three stages of understanding on your own, without the aid of commentaries or study notes. The first several times you read a passage you will probably be confused. This is actually a good thing. Allow yourself to feel lost, to dwell in the "I don't know." It will make the moment of discovery stick.

Nobody likes to feel lost or confused, but it is an important step in the acquisition and retention of understanding. Because of this, I have a few guidelines to lay out for you as you go through this study:

1. **Avoid all commentaries** until comprehension and interpretation have been earnestly attempted on your own. In other words, wait to read commentaries until after you have done the homework, attended

small group time, and listened to the teaching. And then, consult commentaries you can trust. Ask a pastor or Bible teacher at your church for suggested authors.

2. For the purposes of this study, **get a Bible without study notes.** Come on, it's just too easy to look at them. You know I'm right.

3. Though commentaries are off-limits, here are some **tools you should use:**

   - **Cross-references.** These are the Scripture references in the margin or at the bottom of the page in your Bible. They point you to other passages that deal with the same topic or theme.

   - **An English dictionary** to look up unfamiliar words.

   - **Other translations of the Bible.** We will use the English Standard Version (ESV) as a starting point and the New International Version (NIV) as our secondary translation. You can easily consult other versions online. I recommend the NASB or NKJV in addition to the ESV and NIV. Reading a passage in more than one translation can expand your understanding of its meaning. Note: a paraphrase, such as The Message, can be useful but should be regarded as a commentary rather than a translation. Paraphrases are best consulted after careful study of an actual translation.

   - **A printed copy of the text,** double-spaced, so you can mark repeated words, phrases, or ideas. The entire text for this study is provided in the appendix of your Bible study book in the ESV translation.

STORING UP TREASURE

Approaching God's Word with a God-centered perspective, with context, and with care takes effort and commitment. It is study for the long-term. Some days your study may not move you emotionally or speak to an immediate need. You may not be able to apply a passage at all. But what if ten years from now, in a dark night of the soul, that passage suddenly opened up to you because of the work you have done today? Wouldn't your long-term investment be worth it?

In Matthew 13, we see Jesus begin to teach in parables. He tells seven deceptively simple stories that leave His disciples struggling for understanding—dwelling in the "I don't know," if you will. After the last parable He turns to them and asks, "Have you understood all these things?" Despite their apparent confusion, they answer out of their earnest desire with, "Yes." Jesus tells them that their newfound understanding makes them "like the owner of a house who brings out of his storeroom new treasures as well as old" (13:52, NIV).

A storeroom, as Jesus indicates, is a place for keeping valuables over a long period of time for use when needed. Faithful study of God's Word is a means for filling our spiritual storerooms with truth, so that in our hour of need we can bring forth both the old and the new as a source of rich provision. I pray that this study would be for you a source of much treasure, and that you would labor well to obtain it.

Grace and peace,

Jen Wilkin

HOW TO USE THIS STUDY

This Bible study book is designed to be used in a specific way. The homework in the Bible study book will start you down the process of comprehension, interpretation, and application. However, it was designed to dovetail with small group discussion time and the video teachings. You can use the Bible study book by itself, but you are likely to find yourself with some unresolved questions. The video teaching is intended to resolve most, if not all, of your unanswered questions from the homework and discussion time. With this in mind, consider using the materials as follows:

- If you are going through the study on your own, first work through the homework and then watch the corresponding video for that week.

- If you are going through the study in a group, first do your homework, then discuss the questions your group decides to cover, and then watch the teaching.

Note: For Week 1, there is no homework. The study begins with a video introduction. You will find a fill-in sheet on pages 14-15 that you can use as you listen to the introductory material.

HOW TO USE THE LEADER GUIDE

At the end of each week's personal study you will find a leader guide intended to help facilitate discussion in small groups. Each guide begins with an introductory question to help group members get to know each other and feel comfortable contributing their voices to the discussion. These questions may prove to be most helpful during the early weeks of the study, but as the group grows more familiar with one another, group leaders may decide to skip them to allow more time for the questions covering the lesson.

The remainder of the leader guide includes four questions to help group members compare what they have learned from their personal study on Days 2 through 5. These questions are either pulled directly from the personal study or they summarize a concept or theme that the personal study covered. Each two-part question covers content from a particular day of the personal study, first asking group members to reflect and then asking them to apply. The reflection questions typically ask group members to report a finding or flesh out an interpretation. The application questions challenge them to move beyond intellectual understanding to identify ways to live differently in light of what they have learned.

As a small group leader, you will want to review these questions before you meet with your group, thinking through your own answers, marking where they occur in the personal study, and noting if there are any additional questions that you might want to reference to help the flow of the discussion. These questions are suggestions only, intended to help you cover as much ground as you can in a 45-minute discussion time. They should not be seen as requirements or limitations, but as guidelines to help you prepare your group for the teaching time by allowing them to process collectively what they have learned during their personal study.

As a facilitator of discussion rather than a teacher, you are allowed and encouraged to be a colearner with your group members. This means you yourself may not always feel confident of your answer to a given question, and that is perfectly OK. Because we are studying for the long-term, we are allowed to leave some questions partially answered or unresolved, trusting for clarity at a later time. In most cases, the teaching time should address any lingering questions that are not resolved in the personal study or the small group discussion time.

ABOUT THE GOSPEL COALITION

The Gospel Coalition is a fellowship of evangelical churches deeply committed to renewing our faith in the gospel of Christ and to reforming our ministry practices to conform fully to the Scriptures. We have become deeply concerned about some movements within traditional evangelicalism that seem to be diminishing the church's life and leading us away from our historic beliefs and practices. On the one hand, we are troubled by the idolatry of personal consumerism and the politicization of faith; on the other hand, we are distressed by the unchallenged acceptance of theological and moral relativism. These movements have led to the easy abandonment of both biblical truth and the transformed living mandated by our historic faith. We not only hear of these influences, we see their effects. We have committed ourselves to invigorating churches with new hope and compelling joy based on the promises received by grace alone through faith alone in Christ alone.

We believe that in many evangelical churches a deep and broad consensus exists regarding the truths of the gospel. Yet we often see the celebration of our union with Christ replaced by the age-old attractions of power and affluence, or by monastic retreats into ritual, liturgy, and sacrament. What replaces the gospel will never promote a mission-hearted faith anchored in enduring truth working itself out in unashamed discipleship eager to stand the tests of kingdom-calling and sacrifice. We desire to advance along the King's highway, always aiming to provide gospel advocacy, encouragement, and education so that current and next-generation church leaders are better equipped to fuel their ministries with principles and practices that glorify the Savior and do good to those for whom He shed His life's blood.

We want to generate a unified effort among all peoples—an effort that is zealous to honor Christ and multiply His disciples, joining in a true coalition for Jesus. Such a biblically grounded and united mission is the only enduring future for the church. This reality compels us to stand with others who are stirred by the conviction that the mercy of God in Jesus Christ is our only hope of eternal salvation. We desire to champion this gospel with clarity, compassion, courage, and joy—gladly linking hearts with fellow believers across denominational, ethnic, and class lines.

Our desire is to serve the church we love by inviting all our brothers and sisters to join us in an effort to renew the contemporary church in the ancient gospel of Christ so we truly speak and live for Him in a way that clearly communicates to our age. As pastors, we intend to do this in our churches through the ordinary means of His grace: prayer, ministry of the Word, baptism and the Lord's Supper, and the fellowship of the saints. We yearn to work with all who seek the lordship of Christ over the whole of life with unabashed hope in the power of the Holy Spirit to transform individuals, communities, and cultures.

WEEK 1:

1 PETER
INTRODUCTION

Who wrote 1 Peter?

When was it written?

To whom was it written?

In what style was it written?

What are the central themes of the letter?

WEEK 2:

A LIVING HOPE
1 PETER 1:1-12

Each week we will begin our homework by reading through the entire Letter of 1 Peter from start to finish. Then we'll focus in on a particular passage to discover its message and how it fits into the greater context of the letter as a whole. By the time you complete the study, you will have read 1 Peter at least nine times. As it grows more familiar to you, watch for how your understanding expands and deepens. Your first task each week will be to note how this process is taking place. To help you read for detail, you'll also be asked to mark certain words or phrases in the copy of the text in the appendix of this Bible study book. So keep a set of colored pencils handy as you read. If you haven't already, take time to read the introduction to the Bible study book before you start this week's questions.

This week we will focus our efforts on dissecting the first 12 verses of chapter 1. Peter begins his letter with a greeting that does more than introduce the author—it is packed with intentional speech, speech that illuminates the nature of salvation, interweaving New Testament Truth with Old Testament imagery. We'll examine what it means to be "born again," a phrase that is so familiar to us we can lose sight of its miraculous nature. And we'll consider our inheritance as the children of God, both in this life and the next.

DAY ONE

READ 1 PETER FROM BEGINNING TO END.

1. Which section of the letter seems the most unclear to you?

Which section seems the most straightforward?

NOW LOOK BACK AT 1:1-12.

Remember our premise that the Bible is a book about God? We want to know Him better at the end of our study. On Day 1 of each week's homework, we'll take time to read through the text and note everything we learn about God. Your notes might center on one member of the Trinity or the Godhead as a whole. Read asking these questions:

- What is He like?

- What has He done? What is He doing? What will He do?

- What pleases Him? What displeases Him?

2. Do this now for 1:1-12. Some examples have been given to get you started.

The father has foreknowledge about us and all things (1:2).
The Spirit sanctifies us (1:2).
Christ's blood was sprinkled for us (1:2).

3. What do you think Peter wants to communicate in these first 12 verses? Based on what you know from the introductory material, how do his opening lines speak directly to the needs of the people to whom he writes?

DAY TWO

READ 1:1-2.

1. The first two verses of the letter serve as the "envelope" for Peter's message. To whom is Peter writing?

2. On the map to the right, circle the names of each of the regions Peter mentions.

Each of the regions is located in modern-day Turkey. Peter most likely wrote his letter in Rome. His letter would have traveled 1,500 miles to reach the churches to whom he wrote.

How far has his letter traveled to reach you? Google the distance from Rome to your city. _____ miles

We learned last week in our introduction that Peter wrote around 64 A.D. Across how many years has his letter traveled to reach you? _____ years

3. In 1:2, what important doctrine does Peter illustrate in the way he speaks about God? Fill in the blanks below to help with your answer:

according to the foreknowledge of _____
in the sanctification of _____
for obedience to _____ *and for sprinkling of his blood*

important doctrine illustrated here: _____

4. Some of the terms in 1:1-2 deserve our close attention. Read the verses in the ESV and then look up the following words in a dictionary, writing a brief definition for each:

elect (adj):

exile (noun—the verb definition will also be helpful):

dispersion:

foreknow:

sanctification (see also sanctify):

5. Paraphrasing a verse or passage (rewriting it in our own words) can help us to focus on its meaning. It is a useful study tool for a student of the Word. We will use it often in this study. Based on your definitions above, rewrite 1:1-2 in your own words.

6. In what sense are you and I "elect exiles"? How is Peter's letter a letter with our names on the envelope? How do you think his message will be relevant to us 2,000 years later and halfway across the globe?

DAY THREE

NOW LOOK AT 1:3-5.

1. What does it mean to be "born again to a living hope" (1:3)? Look up the following passages and note what each adds to your understanding of this phrase:

   John 1:12-13

   John 3:3-6

   Galatians 4:4-7

2. In what sense is our hope in God a "living hope"? What other forms of hope are there? How is our hope superior to those? Write your thoughts below.

3. What is our living hope (1:4)?
   An _____ that is _____ , _____ ,
   and _____ .

   Where is it kept (1:4)?

4. Look up the following verses and note what each adds to your understanding of the nature of our inheritance in Christ:

   Psalm 16:5-6

   Romans 8:22-25

   1 Corinthians 15:19-26

   Ephesians 1:13-14

   1 John 3:1-3

5. Our inheritance through Christ is imperishable, undefiled, unfading. What are you seeking to inherit in this life? Think about your desires and wants. List some of them below.

   Which of the things above will not perish, spoil, or fade over time? How should this knowledge affect your priorities? Specifically, what priority do you need to change?

6. Rewrite 1:3-5 in your own words.

DAY FOUR

NOW LOOK AT 1:6-9.

1. In 1:6, Peter says "In this you rejoice ..." To what is he referring? In what do we rejoice?

2. What do you think is meant by the phrase "at the revelation of Jesus Christ"(1:7)? Hasn't Christ already been revealed during His incarnation? Look up 1 Corinthians 4:3-5 to help you with your answer.

3. With a green pencil circle every occurrence of the word *revelation* or *revealed* in your copy of the text of 1 Peter (see appendix). Underline the phrase in which it occurs in green. Draw an arrow from the circled word to what was revealed. An example is given below:

   1:5 who by God's power are being guarded through faith for a salvation ready to be revealed in the last time.

   How many occurrences did you find?_____

   Why do you think Peter emphasized this theme to his original readers?

4. What role does Peter say trials play in our lives (1:7)?

Look up the following verses and note what each adds to your understanding of the purpose of trials in our lives:

James 1:2-4

Romans 5:3-4

Romans 8:18 (Note the similarity of Paul's thinking and word choice to Peter's.)

5. Why do you think Peter mentions that his readers have not seen Jesus, nor do they see Him currently in their circumstances? What point does he imply?

6. Does 1:9 teach that we earn our salvation by enduring trials? Give a verse from elsewhere in Scripture to support your answer.

7. What difficult circumstance are you currently facing? How does 1 Peter 1:6-9 apply to your situation?

8. Rewrite 1:6-9 in your own words.

DAY FIVE

NOW LOOK AT 1:10-12.

1. In this passage, what do we learn about the prophets of the Old Testament? Specifically, what do we learn about:

   - The content and purpose of their prophecies?

   - Their method of seeking truth?

   - Their understanding of the prophecies they delivered?

   - Their understanding of an OT prophet's role in the "big picture" of salvation?

2. In 1:12, who does Peter mean by "those who preached the good news to you by the Holy Spirit sent from heaven"?

3. According to 1:12, who gave aid to both the Old Testament prophets and the New Testament preachers of the gospel?

4. Why do you think Peter would tell his original readers that angels long to look into the things they themselves understand about the gospel (1:12)?

   How might this observation be an encouragement to them?

How might it encourage us?

5. In what ways are you challenged to be more like the prophets of old?

Like "those who preach the good news"?

Like the angels described here?

6. Rewrite 1:10-12 in your own words.

WRAP-UP

What impacted you the most within this week's passage of 1 Peter? How has Peter challenged you to look beyond your current circumstances to a future inheritance? How has he encouraged you?

WEEK 2 GROUP DISCUSSION

INTRODUCTORY QUESTION: Have you ever inherited something? If so, what was it?

1. OBSERVE: (question 5, Day 2) Discuss as a group how you wrote 1:1-2 in your own words.

> **APPLY:** (question 6, Day 2) In what sense are you and I "elect exiles"? How do you think Peter's message will be relevant to us 2,000 years later and halfway across the globe?

2. OBSERVE: (question 2, Day 3) In what sense is our hope in God a "living hope"? How is our hope superior to other forms of hope?

> **APPLY:** (question 5, Day 3) Our inheritance through Christ is imperishable, undefiled, unfading. What are you seeking to inherit in this life?

> Which of these things will not perish, spoil, or fade over time? How should this knowledge affect your priorities?

3. OBSERVE: (question 4, Day 4) What role does Peter say trials play in our lives (1:7)?

> **APPLY:** (question 7, Day 4) What difficult circumstance are you currently facing? How does 1 Peter 1:6-9 apply to your situation?

4. OBSERVE: (question 1, Day 5) In 1:10-12, what do we learn about the prophets of the Old Testament?

> **APPLY:** (question 5, Day 5) In what ways are you challenged to be more like the prophets of old? Like "those who preach the good news"? Like the angels described in 1:10-12?

WRAP-UP: What impacted you the most within this week's passage of 1 Peter? How has Peter challenged you to look beyond your current circumstances to a future inheritance? How has he encouraged you?

VIDEO

Now watch the teaching video with your group. After the video concludes, close in prayer. Shape your praise, thanks, confession, and requests around what the Lord has been showing you from 1 Peter this week.

NOTES

_____

_____

_____

_____

_____

_____

_____

_____

_____

_____

_____

_____

_____

_____

WEEK 3:

THE BELIEVER'S IDENTITY
1 PETER 1:13-25

Last week, we saw Peter open his letter by laying out the nature of our future hope, our imperishable and unfading inheritance. We marveled at the fact that we are able to understand the good news we have received in a way not even God's prophets and heaven's angels could comprehend.

This week, Peter will transition from description to prescription. Having described our salvation, Peter will now tell us how we should respond to the good news of grace, even as we endure opposition and trial during our time of exile.

DAY ONE

READ 1 PETER FROM BEGINNING TO END.

1. Has a familiar passage taken on deeper meaning for you with repeated reading this week?

   Has the Holy Spirit brought other passages of Scripture to mind as you read? If so, which ones?

2. We will be marking some repeated words this week on our copy of the text. What words or ideas are you beginning to notice being repeated throughout Peter's letter?

3. Now look back at this week's section of text: 1:13-25. What does this passage teach us about God? Note your observations below:

4. What do you think Peter wants to communicate in 1:13-25? What theme does he continue from the previous section?

DAY TWO

READ 1:13-21, AND THEN FOCUS ON VERSES 13-16.

1. Peter begins this section with an important word. What is it? _____
   What previous idea is he building on?

2. Which of the following forms of holiness is Peter challenging us to
   obediently pursue in 1:13-16? Check all that apply. To the side, note each
   place you found evidence in the text for your answer.

   ☐ holiness in what we think

   ☐ holiness in what we feel

   ☐ holiness in how we act

   Does Peter seem to emphasize one of these three areas of obedience over
   another? Explain your answer.

3. Look up the word *holy* in a dictionary and write a definition for it below
   that best fits the context of 1:13-16.
   holy:

4. In 1:15-16 Peter references a teaching that was familiar to his readers.
   Look up the following verses and note what you find:

   Leviticus 11:44-45

   Leviticus 19:2

   Leviticus 20:7

   Leviticus 20:26

Given that the Book of Leviticus laid out various laws for the nation of Israel, do you think that Peter's exhortation to holiness is a suggestion or a command? What are the implications of your answer?

5. What do the verses above and 1:15-16 indicate should be our motive for pursuing holiness?

Is this always our motive for seeking good conduct, right thinking, and well-governed emotions? Give an example of pursuing a form of holiness from wrong motives.

6. How can we make the holiness of God our motive for pursuing personal holiness? List some practical suggestions below.

7. Rewrite 1:13-16 in your own words.

DAY THREE

NOW LOOK AT 1:17-21.

1. In 1:17, what two descriptions of God are given? _____ and

   _____

   Look up the following verses and note which of these two descriptions they reinforce. Note what additional insight you learn in each text about how God relates to us as Father or Judge.

   Matthew 7:1-2

   Matthew 7:21-23

   Matthew 25:31-46

   Luke 11:11-13

   Luke 15:11-32

   Luke 19:11-27

2. Why do you think Peter refers to God as both Father and Judge, rather than just one or the other?

3. What do you think Peter means by "conduct yourselves with fear throughout the time of your exile" (1:17)? Fear of whom?

4. Look up the word *fear* in the dictionary and write a definition for it below that best fits the context of 1:17—fear of the Lord, our Father and impartial Judge.
   fear:

5. Look up the following verses and note what they teach about fear:
   Proverbs 9:10

   Proverbs 14:26-27

   Proverbs 19:23

   Proverbs 29:25

   Luke 12:4-7

   Luke 12:27-34

6. Where does 1 Peter 1:18 say we learned our futile ways?
   They were _____ from our _____.

7. Compare what you wrote above to 1:3-4. What parallel and contrasting idea do you find?

8. God is both Father and impartial Judge. Is it harder for you to identify with one of these ideas than the other? Why? How does your focus need to shift to bring these two views of God into balance?

9. Rewrite 1:17-19 in your own words.

DAY FOUR

NOW LOOK AT 1:20-21.

1. In the space below, list everything Peter tells you is true about Christ in these two verses.

2. What do you think Peter means by "[he] was made manifest in the last times for the sake of you" (1:20)? Read this verse in the NIV to help you uncover Peter's meaning. You might also look up the word *manifest* (adj.) in a dictionary.

3. Who is the "who" in the phrase "who through him are believers in God" (1:21)?

   Who is the "who" in the phrase "who raised him from the dead and gave him glory" (1:21)?

4. Yesterday we looked at the significance of calling on God the Father as both Father and Judge, in reverent fear. Now let's examine Peter's treatment of God the Son.

   - Scan through your copy of the text, highlighting every occurrence of the name *Jesus* in blue. How many times did it occur in five chapters?

   - Now scan through the text again, highlighting every occurrence of the title *Christ* in yellow. How many times did it occur?

5. The term *Christ* means *the anointed one* and designates the historical person named Jesus as more than just a man. It designates Him as the Messiah foretold of in the Old Testament. It is both a confession of belief and a term of respect.

Look back again at your copy of the text.

- How many times does Peter refer to the Son using both His name (Jesus) and His title of respect (Christ)?

- How many times does Peter refer to the Son using only His title of respect (Christ)?

- How many times does Peter refer to the Son using only His name (Jesus)?

6. What accounts for Peter's choice of address when speaking of Jesus? What does it reveal about his view of the One he left everything to follow?

7. Pretend you expand your highlighting assignment to cover all of the New Testament Epistles (Romans through Jude). Based on what you know of these letters and their authors, would you expect to find a pattern of blue and yellow highlighting that was similar or different to the one you have found here? Why?

8. Now examine your own language when speaking of or to the Savior. If you took a blue highlighter and a yellow highlighter to your own thoughts, prayers, and conversations *about* or *with* Him, what color pattern would emerge? What might it reveal about your view of Him?

9. Rewrite 1:20-21 in your own words.

DAY FIVE

NOW LOOK AT 1:22-25.

1. How does 1:22 say that our souls become purified? Is soul-purification merely the result of praying and receiving?

2. Compare 1:22 to 1:2 and 1:14. Mark the word *obedient/obedience* with an orange O. Do these three verses contain the same idea of obedience or three different aspects of it? Explain your answer.

3. What specific form of obedience is Peter pointing his readers toward in 1:22? How is this a timely reminder for his original audience?

4. Notice how Peter has been developing a theme of *things that last* and *things that perish*. In your copy of the text in the appendix, scan 1:1-25, marking the following words. With a red pencil mark the words *perish* or *perishable* with a capital P. With a purple pencil, mark the word *imperishable* and any synonyms with a capital I.

5. In the columns below, note what Peter has told us is perishable (temporary) and what is imperishable (eternal) in 1:1-25:

Perishable	Imperishable
	Our inheritance (v. 4)

6. What two words are used to describe the Word of God in 1:23? Write them below and note how each expands your understanding of the value of God's Word.

7. In 1:24-25, Peter quotes from an Old Testament passage that would have been familiar to Jewish ears. What is the source of the Scripture he quotes?

8. How is it an appropriate choice to support his topic?

9. What perishable things are most likely to demand your attention and affections? List several below.

How does a focus on those things diminish your ability to love others earnestly from a pure heart?

10. Rewrite 1:22-25 in your own words.

WRAP-UP

What impacted you the most within this week's passage of 1 Peter? How has Peter challenged you to pursue what lasts and put away sin? How has he encouraged you?

WEEK 3 GROUP DISCUSSION

INTRODUCTORY QUESTION: What was your favorite childhood meal?

1. **OBSERVE:** (question 5, Day 2) What does 1:15-16 indicate should be our motive for pursuing holiness? Is this always our motive for seeking good conduct, right thinking, and well-governed emotions? Give an example of pursuing a form of holiness for wrong motives.

   APPLY: (question 6, Day 2) How can we make the holiness of God our motive for pursuing personal holiness?

2. **OBSERVE:** (question 2, Day 3) Why do you think Peter refers to God as both Father and Judge, rather than just one or the other?

   APPLY: (question 8, Day 3) God is both Father and impartial Judge. Is it harder for you to identify with one of these ideas than the other? Why? How does your focus need to shift to bring these two views of God into balance?

3. **OBSERVE:** (questions 4-5, Day 4) What did your highlighting exercise reveal to you about how Peter viewed Jesus?

   APPLY: (question 8, Day 4) Now examine your own language when speaking of or to the Savior. If you took a blue highlighter and a yellow highlighter to your own thoughts, prayers, and conversations about or with Him, what color pattern would emerge? What might it reveal about your view of Him?

4. **OBSERVE:** (question 5, Day 5) In 1:1-25, what does Peter note is perishable (temporary)? What does he note is imperishable (eternal)?

   APPLY: (question 9, Day 5) What perishable things are most likely to demand your attention and affections? How does a focus on those things diminish your ability to love others earnestly from a pure heart?

WRAP-UP: What impacted you most within this week's passage of 1 Peter? How has Peter challenged you to pursue what lasts and put away sin? How has he encouraged you?

VIDEO

Now watch the teaching video with your group. After the video concludes, close in prayer. Shape your praise, thanks, confession, and requests around what the Lord has been showing you from 1 Peter this week.

NOTES

_____

_____

_____

_____

_____

_____

_____

_____

_____

_____

_____

_____

_____

WEEK 4:

LIVING STONES
1 PETER 2:1-12

Last week, Peter contrasted the perishable nature of man and the imperishable seed of salvation. In response to the knowledge of our future hope, even in the midst of difficulty, we seek to hope fully in grace, be holy as God is holy, conduct ourselves with reverent fear, and love earnestly.

This week, Peter will offer encouragement about how to live as a holy people. He will help his hearers understand the importance of their relationships to Christ and to each other, as well as the importance of being a witness to an unbelieving world.

DAY ONE

READ 1 PETER FROM BEGINNING TO END.

1. Has a familiar passage taken on deeper meaning for you with repeated reading this week?

2. Has the Holy Spirit brought other passages of Scripture to mind as you read? If so, which ones?

3. Now look back at this week's section of text: 2:1-12. What does this passage teach us about God?

4. What main idea do you think Peter wants to communicate in 2:1-12?

5. How does this section fit with Peter's objective to encourage his readers in the face of difficulty?

DAY TWO

NOW LOOK AT 2:1-3.

1. What does the first word of 2:1 tell us about what Peter is about to say?

   How does the idea in this section flow from the previous one?

2. We may be tempted to rush through the rich vocabulary Peter has chosen in 2:1. Let's look up definitions for each of these carefully selected words.

   malice:

   deceit:

   hypocrisy:

   envy:

   slander:

3. Which of these sins do you need to "put away"? Take some time to examine your thoughts, speech, and actions. Write below at least one specific relationship you want to improve by putting away these sins.

4. Use a thesaurus to come up with antonyms for each of the words you defined. In the space below, rewrite 2:1 using the antonyms so that it says "do" instead of "don't":

So clothe yourself in all _____ and all _____ and _____ and _____ and all _____.

How would following this command alter the relationship(s) you listed in question 3? Stop and pray for each relationship before moving on to the next question.

5. Notice how Peter has been developing a theme of salvation and rebirth. In your copy of the text, scan through 1:1-2:3. With a blue pencil, mark the words *salvation* and *born again* with a capital S.

6. What do you think Peter means by "that you may grow up into salvation" (2:2)? Read this verse in the NASB and NKJV to help with your answer.

7. Rewrite 2:1-3 in your own words.

DAY THREE

NOW LOOK AT 2:4-8.

1. What image does Peter use to describe Christ and Christians in 2:4-5?

   _____ _____

   Note how this image builds on his words from earlier sections of the letter:
   1:3 "he has caused us to be born again to a _____
   _____"
   1:23 "you have been born again, not of perishable seed
   but of imperishable, through the _____ and
   abiding _____ ___ _____"

2. What Old Testament parallel does Peter want to bring to mind through images like *spiritual house, holy priesthood,* and *spiritual sacrifices*? Why do you think he wants to make this connection?

3. In what ways does the body of believers function as a spiritual house? What is the parallel to the Old Testament temple Peter wants us to understand? Read Exodus 25:1-22 (I like it in the NIV personally) and note as many parallels as you can find.

4. We will talk about the significance of being a holy priesthood in the homework for Day 4. What spiritual sacrifices can believers offer to God? Look up the following verses to help with your answer.
   Psalm 51:17

   Romans 12:1

   Romans 15:15-16

   Hebrews 13:15-16

5. Four types of "stone" metaphors are applied to Jesus in this passage—one is Peter's, noted in question 1, and three come from Old Testament passages he quotes (Ps. 118:22; Isa. 8:13-15; Isa. 28:16). Note each metaphor next to its reference in 1 Peter. Note the OT reference, if applicable. Using a dictionary to help you, explain why each metaphor describes Jesus well.

   2:4

   2:6

   2:7 *(read in the NIV to catch the difference in vocabulary)*

   2:8

6. What do you think is meant by the phrase "and whoever believes in him will not be put to shame" (2:6b)?

7. What do you think is meant by the phrase "they stumble because they disobey the word, as they were destined to do" (2:8b)? Who is "they"? Look at Romans 9:30-33 to see if Paul can help you with your answer.

8. Like Christ, what kinds of rejection have you faced as a "living stone"? How does such rejection shape your understanding of what it means to follow Him? Of what it means to enjoy fellowship with other "living stones"?

9. Rewrite 2:4-8 in your own words.

DAY FOUR

NOW LOOK AT 2:9-10.

1. In these two verses, Peter gives six different descriptions of who we are as believers. List them below:

   1.

   2.

   3.

   4.

   5.

   6.

NOW LET'S EXAMINE EACH OF THESE AND HOW IT IMPACTS OUR RELATIONSHIPS AND ROLES.

2. Peter says believers are a "chosen race." Look back through the text we have studied thus far, marking every occurrence of the word *chosen* with an orange circle. Below, note how the knowledge that you are part of a chosen people affects your relationship with (and thoughts and actions toward):
   God

   other believers

   unbelievers

3. Peter says believers are a "royal priesthood." Think about what you know of the OT priesthood, its duties and requirements. We will examine this further in the teaching time, but for now, think about how the priesthood was set apart to offer sacrifices on behalf of the people and to honor God as God. Below, note how the knowledge that you are part of a royal priesthood affects your relationship with (and thoughts and actions toward):

   God

   other believers

   unbelievers

4. Peter says believers are a "holy nation," a people for God's own possession. Think about what strives to gain possession of you in this world. Below, note how the knowledge that you are His possession affects your relationship with (and thoughts and actions toward):

   God

   other believers

   unbelievers

5. Peter says of believers in 2:10: "Once you were not a people, but now you are God's people; once you had not received mercy, but now you have received mercy." Is this thought a reiteration of what he has said previously, or does it communicate a new idea? Does it remind you of a line from "Amazing Grace" at all? Below, note how the idea of having been transformed affects your relationship with (and thoughts and actions toward):

God

other believers

unbelievers

6. Rewrite 2:9-10 in your own words.

DAY FIVE

NOW LOOK AT 2:11-12. READ IT IN THE ESV AND NIV.

1. Look up the following words in a dictionary to help you understand Peter's meaning.
   exile (see Week 1, Day 2):

   sojourner (sojourn):

   abstain:

   passions:

2. How many times has Peter mentioned "exiles" in his letter up to this point? _____ How does his addition of the word *sojourners* expand your understanding of a believer's relationship to the world around her?

3. Look up the following verses and note what they add to your understanding of exiles and sojourners, and what it means to live like they do.
   Luke 12:32-34

   2 Corinthians 5:1,20

   2 Corinthians 5:6-9

   Philippians 3:20-21

4. Give some examples of what Peter might have in mind with the term "passions of the flesh." How would remembering that you are an exile and a sojourner help you to do battle with these passions?

5. What reason does Peter give for living honorable lives among the Gentiles (unbelievers)?

6. Have you ever given up a behavior, pastime, or preference because it could send the wrong message to an unbeliever? Has the Lord been showing you anything you need to set aside? Pray and ask that He would keep you more interested in His glory than your desires or comfort.

7. Rewrite 2:11-12 in your own words.

WRAP-UP

What impacted you the most within this week's passage of 1 Peter? How has Peter challenged you to look beyond your current circumstances to a future inheritance? How has he encouraged you?

WEEK 4 GROUP DISCUSSION

INTRODUCTORY QUESTION: What is the most memorable building you have ever visited?

1. **OBSERVE:** (question 4a, Day 2) Discuss the antonyms you choose for each of the words in 1 Peter 2:1. Share your rewritten verse with the group:

   So clothe yourself in all_____ **and all** _____
   and _____**and** _____
   and all_____.

   APPLY: (question 4b, Day 2) How would following this "do" command alter our primary relationships?

2. **OBSERVE:** (question 5, Day 3) How does each of the four "stone" metaphors found in 2:4-8 describe Jesus well?

   APPLY: (question 8, Day 3) Like Christ, what kinds of rejection have you faced as a "living stone"? How does such rejection shape your understanding of what it means to follow Him? Of what it means to enjoy fellowship with other "living stones"?

3. **OBSERVE:** (questions 2-5, Day 4) Which of the four different ideas in each of these questions (chosen people, royal priesthood, God's possession, transformed by mercy) stood out to you as most remarkable? Why?

   APPLY: (questions 2-5, Day 4) How does knowing you are each of those four things affect your relationship with (and thoughts and actions toward) God, other believers, and unbelievers?

4. **OBSERVE:** (question 5, Day 5) What reason does Peter give for living honorable lives among the Gentiles (unbelievers)?

   APPLY: (question 6, Day 5) Have you ever given up a behavior, pastime, or preference because it could send the wrong message to an unbeliever? Has the Lord been showing you anything you need to set aside?

WRAP-UP: What impacted you most within this week's passage of 1 Peter? How has Peter challenged you to look beyond your current circumstances to a future inheritance? How has he encouraged you?

VIDEO

Now watch the teaching video with your group. After the video concludes, close in prayer. Shape your praise, thanks, confession, and requests around what the Lord has been showing you from 1 Peter this week.

NOTES

_____

_____

_____

_____

_____

_____

_____

_____

_____

_____

_____

_____

_____

_____

WEEK 5:

SUBMISSION – PART 1

1 PETER 2:13-25

Last week, we learned the importance of craving the milk of the Word. Peter urged us to retrain our appetites, to see ourselves as part of a living temple, and to recognize the great privilege of our position as a chosen people. He stressed the importance of living exemplary lives among the lost for the sake of our witness.

This week, Peter will begin explaining the nature of submission. We will spend three weeks developing our understanding of what submission is, to whom we are called to submit, and why submission is not the same thing as weakness. We begin with the call to submit to human institutions and earthly masters.

DAY ONE

READ 1 PETER FROM BEGINNING TO END.

1. Has a familiar passage taken on deeper meaning for you with repeated reading this week?

   Has the Holy Spirit brought other passages of Scripture to mind as you read? If so, which ones?

2. Now look back at this week's section of text: 2:13-25. What does this passage teach us about God?

3. What main idea do you think Peter wants to communicate in 2:13-25?

4. How does this section fit with Peter's objective to encourage his readers in the face of difficulty?

5. Look back at 2:11-12. How does this week's section flow logically from the previous one?

DAY TWO

LOOK AT 2:13-17. READ IT IN THE ESV AND NIV. WE WILL DIVIDE OUR STUDY OF THIS SECTION BETWEEN DAY 2 AND DAY 3.

1. What word does the NIV use to translate "Be subject to" in 2:13?

   Where else in 2:13–3:7 does this word occur?

   Look up *submit* in the dictionary and write a definition for it below that best fits the context of its usage in this passage.
   submit (verb, intransitive):

2. Why do you think the idea of submission causes so much controversy inside and outside the church today? What negative stereotypes are associated with submissive people?

3. How would you respond to the charge that submissiveness is a negative trait?

4. What reasons does Peter give for submitting ourselves to human authorities?

2:13

2:15

How do these reasons affect the way the believer thinks about submission to governing authorities?

5. What motives that are not "for the Lord's sake" might someone have for submitting to governing authorities?

6. Look at 2:15. What do foolish people think about submission to authority? How does their foolishness give an opportunity to the believer to be an example?

7. How does living in a democracy impact our thinking about submission to governing authorities? Does it make submission easier or more difficult? Explain your answer.

DAY THREE

1. What kind of freedom does Peter have in view in 2:16? What has the believer been freed from? What has she been freed to? Look up 1 Corinthians 9:19-23 to help with your answer.

2. How does Peter intend us to use our freedom to honor God?

   How might we be tempted to use freedom to cover evil?

3. How should "living as servants of God" affect the way we submit to others (2:16)?

4. What is Peter's point in 2:17?

Peter is not the only New Testament writer who talks about how to relate to governing authorities. Paul spends some time on the topic as well. Both men had more than their share of tense moments with those in governmental authority over them. Ultimately, both would submit to governmental authority to the point of martyrdom.

5. Look up Romans 13:1-7 and note what Paul adds to Peter's thoughts on submission to governing authorities. What reasons does he give for our submission?

List everything Paul notes that we should give these authorities as their due (13:7).

Which of these things is most difficult for you to give? Why?

6. Look up the passages below to see instances of Peter, Jesus, and Paul interacting with the Jewish authorities. You might want to read a little of what leads up to each passage to get your bearings. In light of our discussion of submission, how do you explain their behavior in these scenes? Are they submissive? Why or why not?
John 18:19-23

Acts 4:18-20

Acts 5:27-29

Acts 23:1-5

7. What governing authority do you least want to submit to? The IRS? The president? Your neighborhood association? Write the name of the person or governing body below. What does your unwillingness to submit reveal about your heart? Ask the Lord to soften your heart, so that your submission to human authority becomes an extension of your submission to Him.

8. Rewrite 2:13-17 in your own words.

DAY FOUR

NOW LOOK AT 2:18-25. READ IT IN THE ESV AND NIV. WE WILL DIVIDE OUR STUDY OF THIS SECTION BETWEEN DAY 4 AND DAY 5.

1. To whom is Peter addressing his comments in this section? To whom might his comments apply today?

2. What does Peter say is due to those in authority over us, regardless of whether they are just or unjust in their leadership (2:18)?

   _____   _____

   Think of someone whose unjust leadership you do not enjoy submitting to. Do you give that person all respect, both publicly and privately? What does giving all respect entail in thought, word, and deed? What does it not entail?

3. What is Peter's train of thought in 2:19-20? What point is he making?

4. Read Luke 6:27-36. Who is speaking? What similar ideas are spoken here?

5. What reasons for enduring harsh treatment does Peter give in 2:21-25?

6. What behaviors of Christ does Peter highlight for us to follow as our example?

7. Look up Philippians 2:5-7. In what way does this passage say Christ emptied Himself?

Now look up Matthew 5:2-3. What does Christ teach is true about those who follow His example to empty themselves?

Pray and ask God that you would desire to be emptied as Christ was, that the blessings of servanthood may fill you to overflowing.

DAY FIVE

1. Now let's focus in on one particular aspect of Jesus' response to unjust treatment. Look at 2:23 in the NIV. In the face of injustice, what did Jesus refrain from doing? Instead, what did He do?

   "he _____ _____ to him who judges justly."

   Now look at the same phrase in the ESV. How does it expand your understanding of how Jesus responded?

2. What does it mean to entrust yourself to the One who judges justly? Take some time to meditate on the idea of God as the just Judge. Look up the verses below and draw a line to match them to the thought they contain.

Isaiah 33:22	He cannot be swayed by a person's status. He is impartial.
Acts 10:34-35	He cannot be bribed.
1 Samuel 2:10	He not only judges by the Law, He is the author (giver) of the Law.
Hebrews 4:13	He will judge every one of us on earth.
Jeremiah 17:10	He is not swayed by outward appearances.
1 Samuel 16:7b	He cannot be coerced/convinced.
Isaiah 40:13-14	Nothing and no one is hidden from His sight.
Psalm 50:10-12	He is able to judge not just actions, but thoughts and motives.

3. Based on the verses above, in what ways is God like an earthly judge who presides in a courtroom? In what ways is He more trustworthy than any earthly judge?

4. What reason is given in 2:24 for Jesus' death on the tree? How does this reason instruct us in our response to unjust suffering?

5. In 2:24b-25, what famous Old Testament prophecy does Peter paraphrase? Find the cross-reference and look up the passage. Read the entire chapter and note any key phrases or ideas that are echoed by Peter in 2:18-25.

6. Have you ever had an unjust master? Someone whose decision-making was unfair or dishonest? Someone who caused you hurt though you had done nothing to deserve it? How do you think Jesus would have responded in that situation? How would His view of Himself in relation to the Father and others affect His response?

7. Rewrite 2:18-25 in your own words.

WRAP-UP

What impacted you the most within this week's passage of 1 Peter? How has Peter challenged you to look beyond your current circumstances to a future inheritance? What are the words of Peter asking of you personally?

WEEK 5 GROUP DISCUSSION

INTRODUCTORY QUESTION: What traffic law are you most likely to break? Why?

1. **OBSERVE:** (question 6, Day 2) Based on 2:15, what do foolish people think about submission to authority? How does their foolishness give an opportunity to the believer to be an example?

   APPLY: (question 7, Day 2) How does living in a democracy impact our thinking about submission to governing authorities? Does it make submission easier or harder? Explain your answer.

2. **OBSERVE:** (question 3, Day 3) How should "living as servants of God" affect the way we submit to others (2:16)?

   APPLY: (question 7, Day 3) What governing authority do you least want to submit to? The IRS? The president? Your neighborhood association? What does your unwillingness to submit reveal about your heart?

3. **OBSERVE:** (question 1, Day 4) To whom is Peter addressing his comments in 2:18-25? To whom might his comments apply today?

   APPLY: (question 2, Day 4) Think of someone whose unjust leadership you do not enjoy submitting to. Do you give that person all respect, both publicly and privately (2:18)? What does giving all respect entail in thought, word, and deed? What does it not entail?

4. **OBSERVE:** (question 3, Day 5) In what ways is God like an earthly judge who presides in a courtroom? In what ways is He more trustworthy than any earthly judge?

   APPLY: (question 6, Day 5) Have you ever had an unjust master? How do you think Jesus would have responded in that situation? How would His view of Himself in relation to the Father and others affect His response?

WRAP-UP: What impacted you most within this week's passage of 1 Peter? How has Peter challenged you to look beyond your current circumstances to a future inheritance? What are the words of Peter asking of you personally?

VIDEO

Now watch the teaching video with your group. After the video concludes, close in prayer. Shape your praise, thanks, confession, and requests around what the Lord has been showing you from 1 Peter this week.

NOTES

_____

_____

_____

_____

_____

_____

_____

_____

_____

_____

_____

_____

WEEK 6:

SUBMISSION - PART 2
1 PETER 3:1-12

Last week, Peter opened his discussion of submission by addressing our responsibility to human institutions and masters. We noted that submission is willingly placing yourself under someone else's leadership. It is not subjugation, nor is it weakness. Biblical submission is about meekness, or strength under control, shown clearly to us in the example of Christ.

This week, Peter addresses the issue of submission within marriage. Take a deep breath. I know this can be a scary topic for women, and one that is often taught without nuance or context. If you have never studied these passages in the context of the rest of Peter's letter, I think you will find freedom in doing so. We will give the text our full attention in the interest of banishing cultural ideas and embracing biblical ones.

DAY ONE

READ 1 PETER FROM BEGINNING TO END.

1. Choose a passage from the text that has already had an impact on your relationships or your perspective. Spend some time committing the beginning of your chosen passage to memory.

2. Now look back at this week's section of text: 3:1-12. What does this passage teach us about God?

3. What do you think Peter wants to communicate in 3:1-12? Boil down his point to three or four bullet points.

4. How does this section flow logically out of the previous one?

DAY TWO

NOW LOOK AT 3:1-6. READ IT IN THE ESV AND NIV.

Wouldn't it be great to just skip this part?

Not a chance. Far better to look at Peter's instructions to wives in context. Far better to know exactly what is said and not said in this passage, so that we do not fall prey to false teaching that runs to one extreme or the other.

The issue of submission in marriage has been the source of much contention within and outside the church. We will cover it at some length during the teaching this week. As you probably noted in your dictionary definition, submission is the willing act of yielding to the authority of another. This is what Christ did on the cross: He willingly yielded to the will of the Father.

For wives, submission is an act of faith: faith that God is working through her husband to accomplish what is best for her. Admittedly, more faith is required of some wives than of others in this matter. But the principle remains that God never asks of us something that is for our spiritual harm. With this mindset, let's approach the topic at hand.

1. How do unbelievers tend to stereotype the submissive wife in a negative light? How does she think, speak, act, and dress? Complete the statements below.
   The ridiculously submissive Christian wife always …

   The ridiculously submissive Christian wife never …

2. How do well-meaning believers tend to stereotype the submissive wife as a glorious ideal? How does she think, speak, act, and dress? Complete the statements below.
   The beautifully submissive Christian wife always …

   The beautifully submissive Christian wife never …

3. What is your own perception of what it means and does not mean to be a submissive wife? Don't worry about "getting the right answer" here, just be honest.

NOW LET'S TURN TO THE TEXT. LOOK AT 3:1-2.

4. What is the first word of 3:1? _____ What is its significance? Explain the parallel relationship Peter is drawing between this passage and the previous one.

5. Marriage is a human institution ordained by God. What is the first and foremost reason a wife should strive to willingly submit to her husband's leadership? Look back at 2:13 to help with your answer.

6. How does Peter say the unbelieving husband may be won to faith (3:1)? What common misconception is Peter asking wives to set aside?

7. At first glance, it appears that a wife's respectful and pure conduct toward her husband is what will influence him. Read 3:2 in both the ESV and NIV. What bigger idea does Peter point toward?

8. What wisdom does 3:1-2 offer to wives of unbelievers? To wives of believers? Is there any wisdom here for unmarried women as well?

We'll continue on this topic tomorrow. For now, pray and ask God to help you have ears to hear what He has for you in this section of 1 Peter. Ask Him to help you set aside either the bias of culture or the bias of bad teaching. Ask Him for the freedom that comes from submitting to His will.

DAY THREE

CONTINUING IN OUR STUDY OF 3:1-6, NOW LOOK AT VERSES 3-6.

1. What is Peter saying in 3:3-4? Is he suggesting that truly godly women don't wear makeup, fix their hair, or accessorize?

2. What significant word does Peter use to describe the beauty of a gentle and quiet spirit (3:4)? _____ Mark this word in your text as you have before, with a purple I.

   What phrase is used in the NIV?

   What contrast is Peter establishing between physical and spiritual beauty?

3. What practices or disciplines enhance physical beauty? List all that you can think of below. Think about your weekly schedule. How many hours of your week are spent preserving or enhancing physical beauty? Think about your body from head to toe and add up approximately how many hours a week you spend cleaning, grooming, toning, clothing, or painting it. If you work out, be honest about whether you do so for fitness or for appearance.

4. What practices or disciplines enhance spiritual beauty? List all that you can think of below.

How many hours of your week are spent preserving or enhancing the imperishable beauty of a gentle and quiet spirit?

5. What woman is given as our example in 3:5-6? _____ We will discuss her story in the teaching time, but for now, note below any thoughts you have on why Peter singles her out as an example to wives. You can look back to her story in Genesis 12–23 if you would like.

6. Look back at last week's lesson, question 6, Day 3. As we noted in the lesson, did Peter, Jesus, and Paul always submit to the governing authorities?

Likewise (3:1), can you think of any examples where a wife would not be bound to submit to her husband's authority? List your thoughts below.

7. How might the recognition that submission to your husband is not required in every situation protect you?

How might that recognition be a temptation to sin for you?

8. Rewrite 3:1-6 in your own words.

DAY FOUR

NOW LOOK AT 3:7. READ IT IN THE ESV AND NIV.

1. What is the first word of 3:7? _____ What is its significance? Explain the parallel relationship Peter is drawing between this passage and the previous one.

2. How are husbands commanded to live with their wives? Explain what you think Peter means. Give examples.

3. What two reasons does Peter give for husbands to treat their wives respectfully?

4. How does the NIV translate the phrase "showing honor to the woman as the weaker vessel"?

5. Peter is indicating that women are weaker than men in some respects. What kind(s) of weakness do you think Peter has in view here?
   - ☐ Physical weakness
   - ☐ Emotional weakness
   - ☐ Intellectual weakness
   - ☐ Spiritual weakness

Do you agree with his statement? Is he making a general statement (a statement that is generally true) or a definitive one (a statement that is true in all cases)?

6. How should the phrase "they are heirs with you of the grace of life" instruct a husband? How should it affect a husband's thoughts, words, and actions?

7. How many verses did Peter devote to instructing slaves (look back at chapter 2)? _____ wives? _____ husbands? _____ Why do you think his writing is structured this way?

8. Rewrite 3:7 in your own words.

DAY FIVE

LOOK AT 3:8-12.

1. What is the first word of 3:8? _____ What does it tell
   you about what Peter is about to say? Is he introducing a new topic?

   To whom are his comments in 3:8-12 addressed?

2. Peter lists five things we need to have to be able to relate rightly to
   one another. Write each of them below, along with a brief explanation.
   Use the NIV and a dictionary to help you.
   1.

   2.

   3.

   4.

   5.

   Which of these things is hardest for you to demonstrate to other
   believers? Which is easiest? Why?

3. What rule for living does Peter give in 3:9? How does the passage
   he quotes in 3:10-12 reinforce his thought?

4. Rewrite 3:8-12 in your own words.

5. As we wrap up this week, let's get a look at the big picture on submission. The chart below contains references for the three main places submission is addressed in the New Testament: Ephesians 5, Colossians 3, and our text for this week in 1 Peter 2–3. Summarize briefly what each passage has to say.

	1 Peter 2:13–3:8	Ephesians 5:15–6:9	Colossians 3:12-25
Wives	3:1-6 be subject to husbands, respectful, quiet, gentle spirit	5:22-24,33b	3:18
Husbands	3:7	5:25-33	3:19
Slaves	2:18-25	6:5-8	3:22
Everyone	2:13-17; 3:8	5:15-21	3:12-17,23-25

We will discuss this chart during the teaching time. But for now, how has a broader examination of what Scripture says about submission added to your understanding of the issue?

WRAP-UP

What impacted you the most within this week's passage of 1 Peter? How has Peter challenged your view of what it means to submit to authority? What are the words of Peter asking of you personally?

WEEK 6 GROUP DISCUSSION

INTRODUCTORY QUESTION: Who are your favorite TV husband and wife? Why?

1. **OBSERVE:** (question 6, Day 2) How does Peter say the unbelieving husband may be won to faith (3:1)? What common misconception is Peter asking wives to set aside?

   APPLY: (question 8, Day 2) What wisdom does 3:1-2 offer to wives of unbelievers? To wives of believers? Is there any wisdom here for unmarried women as well?

2. **OBSERVE:** (question 6, Day 3) Can you think of any examples where a wife would not be bound to submit to her husband's authority?

   APPLY: (question 7, Day 3) How might the recognition that submission to your husband is not required in every situation protect you? How might that recognition be a temptation to sin for you?

3. **OBSERVE:** (question 2, Day 4) How are husbands commanded to live with their wives (3:7)? Explain what you think Peter means. Give examples.

   APPLY: (question 6, Day 4) How should the phrase "they are heirs with you of the grace of life" instruct a husband? How should it affect a husband's thoughts, words, and actions?

4. **OBSERVE:** (question 2a, Day 5) In 3:8-12, Peter lists five things we need to have to be able to relate rightly to one another. What are they? Give a brief explanation of each one.

   APPLY: (question 2b, Day 5) Which of these five things is hardest for you to demonstrate to other believers? Which is easiest? Why?

WRAP-UP: What impacted you most within this week's passage of 1 Peter? How has Peter challenged your view of what it means to submit to authority? What are the words of Peter asking of you personally?

VIDEO

Now watch the teaching video with your group. After the video concludes, close in prayer. Shape your praise, thanks, confession, and requests around what the Lord has been showing you from 1 Peter this week.

NOTES

_____

_____

_____

_____

_____

_____

_____

_____

_____

_____

_____

WEEK 7:

SUBMISSION
– PART 3
1 PETER 3:13-22

Last week, we examined Peter's words about submission within marriage. We discussed how the historical and cultural context shape our understanding of how the believer should show honor to a spouse, particularly an unbelieving one. Peter removes all doubt that submission is a topic for women only. Every believer is called to submit.

This week, Peter will round out his thoughts on submission by describing how to submit even in the midst of persecution. How should the believer respond to suffering that results from doing good? Our passage this week contains one of the most difficult texts in the New Testament, so bring your study skills. We'll work to gain some ownership over a few verses we may usually move past as quickly as possible. And we'll end with a vision of authority and submission that will make the work worthwhile.

DAY ONE

READ 1 PETER FROM BEGINNING TO END.

1. As you read, underline in red every occurrence of the word *suffer/suffered/suffering* with a jagged line. How many sections of Peter's letter address suffering? _____

2. Spend some time committing to memory the verses you chose on Day 1 of last week.

3. Now look back at this week's section of text: 3:13-22. What does this passage teach us about God?

4. What do you think Peter wants to communicate in 3:13-22? Summarize his point in three or four bullet points.

5. How does this section flow logically out of the previous one?

DAY TWO

LOOK AT 3:13-14A.

1. At first glance, what would seem to be the answer to Peter's question in 3:13?

2. Specifically, what kind of suffering is Peter talking about in 3:14? What assurance does he give his listeners?

3. When might doing good keep us from being persecuted? When might it cause us to be persecuted? Give an example of each situation.

4. By doing good all the time, could we hope to avoid all persecution? Look up 2 Timothy 3:12 to help with your answer.

5. When he says, "Have no fear of them, nor be troubled" (3:14b), Peter paraphrases Isaiah 8:12-13. Look up these verses and note the complete thought that Isaiah speaks. How do these verses add to your understanding of Peter's meaning?

6. How does our fear of the Lord affect our fear of persecution?

7. Look up Matthew 5:10-12 and note whose teaching Peter is paraphrasing in 3:13-14a. What similarities do you see between the two passages?

8. Both Peter and Jesus say that when we are persecuted we will be blessed. In what ways might someone persecuted for her faith experience blessing in the midst of her suffering? Has this ever been your experience?

DAY THREE

NOW LOOK AT 3:14B-17.

1. In the chart below, note in the appropriate column every instruction Peter gives for our behavior under persecution:

Heart	Mind	Speech	Actions

2. Looking at your answers above, how do the inward behaviors of the heart and mind shape the outward behaviors of speech and actions?

3. What do you think Peter means by "in your hearts honor Christ the Lord as holy" (3:15)? Look at how the NIV translates this phrase to help with your answer.

4. What steps can we take to be prepared to make a defense of our faith? Think of three practices that would help us to be prepared.

5. Would you be ready to make a defense of your faith if you were called to do so? Would you be ready if you knew you or your family would be put at risk because of your words?

6. What is the difference between giving a defense and being defensive (3:15)? How hard is it to separate these ideas when you are under verbal attack? How would you advise someone to "keep her cool" when her belief is questioned?

7. Peter says to defend your belief with gentleness and respect. Is this our usual demeanor when answering an opposing view? How might following Peter's advice leave you with a good conscience?

8. Look up Proverbs 15:1. What other good reason for gentleness and respectful speech is found here?

9. Now look at what Paul says on this topic. Note how his instructions about speaking to unbelievers expand on Peter's instructions in 3:15-16. *Colossians 4:5-6*

   2 Timothy 2:24-26

10. Have you ever been persecuted for doing good or defending your faith? How was your faith affected by that experience? How were your words or actions affected?

11. Rewrite 3:13-17 in your own words.

DAY FOUR

NOW LOOK AT 3:18-22.

This is a famously (and obviously) difficult passage to understand, so let's find a way to examine it that makes sense.

1. Before we put the passage under the microscope, let's look at it from outer space. What is the big idea Peter wants to communicate in 3:18-22? What does he want us to know Christ accomplished? Keep in mind Peter's purpose in writing this letter: to encourage those enduring suffering. Also, keep in mind what Peter just talked about in 3:13-17.

Now let's get more detailed. We'll take a closer look at 3:18 today, and then we'll tackle 3:19-22 in tomorrow's homework.

2. How does the thought in 3:18 flow logically from the thought in 3:17?

3. Why did Christ die on the cross (3:18)?

4. Why does Peter say "Christ also suffered *once* for sins" (3:18, emphasis mine)? Read Hebrews 10:5-14 to help with your answer.

5. On Day 1 of this week, you marked every occurrence of the word *suffer* in the book of 1 Peter with a jagged red underline. Peter addresses not just the way followers of Christ suffer, but the way Christ Himself suffered. Look up the following verses and note how they shape your understanding of the purpose of suffering.

Hebrews 5:7-8
Jesus learned _____ through what He suffered.

Hebrews 2:10
Jesus was made _____ (purified) through suffering.

2 Corinthians 12:7
Paul was allowed to suffer to keep him from becoming _____.

2 Corinthians 1:3-6
Sharing in suffering allows us to also share in _____.

6. Which of the above benefits have you found to be true in your own experience of suffering? Stop to pray and thank God for the good He has brought out of suffering in your life. Ask Him to give you assurance that current and future suffering are for your good.

DAY FIVE

1. What has been the overarching theme of our study for the past three weeks? (Glance at the table of contents if you need help.)

In your opinion, does 3:18-22 continue this theme or move on to another one? Give reasons from the text for your answer.

Now let's see if we can make sense of 3:19-22.

2. At this point in the study, you have read 3:19-20 multiple times. What is your best guess as to what these verses mean?

3. In 3:19, what does "in which" refer back to? Who went and proclaimed to the spirits in prison?

4. There are several possible explanations for who these "spirits in prison" are. We will discuss them further during the teaching, but for now, here is a summary of the more common ones:

- The spirits are disobedient humans who lived in the time of Noah, now in hell, whom Jesus proclaimed the gospel to between His death and resurrection.

- The spirits are the disobedient humans of Noah's day, whom Christ preached to *through* Noah before the flood.

- The spirits are fallen angels, who stirred up the wickedness in Noah's day, to whom Christ proclaimed His victory over sin.

Which of these views seems like the best fit to you? Why?

5. Now let's look for some clues within the passage and from other places in Scripture. Compare 3:19-20a to 3:22. What phrase in 3:22 might correspond to "spirits in prison" who "formerly did not obey"?

6. Now look up the following verses and note how they add to your understanding of "spirits in prison."

   Ephesians 6:12

   Colossians 2:15

   2 Peter 2:4 (note also who is referenced in verse 5)

   Jude 1:6

   Revelation 20:1-3,7

   Based on these verses, how would you interpret the meaning of "spirits in prison" who "formerly did not obey"?

7. What does Peter say baptism corresponds to (3:21)?

Think back to what you know of the story of Noah and the ark. What parallels to baptism do you see? (If you need a memory refresher, read Gen. 6:9–9:17.)

8. What is baptism a picture of? Look up the following verses to help with your answer.

Romans 6:4

Colossians 2:12

9. What does Peter mean when he says baptism saves us (3:21)? What does he not mean? Explain your answer.

10. Now reflect over the past three weeks' discussion of submission. What reasons for submitting struck you as the most compelling? How will you change your approach to a key relationship because of what you have learned?

11. Rewrite 3:18-22 in your own words.

WRAP-UP

What impacted you most within this week's passage of 1 Peter? How has Peter challenged your view of what submission looks like? What are the words of Peter asking of you personally?

WEEK 7 GROUP DISCUSSION

INTRODUCTORY QUESTION: Who was your favorite elementary school teacher? Why?

1. **OBSERVE:** (question 4, Day 2) By doing good all the time, could we hope to avoid all persecution? Look up 2 Timothy 3:12 to help with your answer.

   APPLY: (question 8, Day 2) Both Peter and Jesus say that when we are persecuted we will be blessed. In what ways might someone persecuted for her faith experience blessing in the midst of her suffering? Has this ever been your own experience?

2. **OBSERVE:** (question 6, Day 3) What is the difference between giving a defense and being defensive? (3:15) How would you advise someone to "keep her cool" when her belief is questioned?

   APPLY: (question 10, Day 3) Have you ever been persecuted for doing good or defending your faith? How was your faith affected by that experience? How were your words or actions affected?

3. **OBSERVE:** (question 5, Day 4) Peter addresses not just the way followers of Christ suffer, but the way Christ Himself suffered. How did the verses listed with this question shape your understanding of the purpose of suffering?

   APPLY: (question 6, Day 4) Have you found the benefits you've discussed to be true in your own experience of suffering?

4. **OBSERVE:** (question 1, Day 5) In your opinion, does 3:18-22 continue the theme of submission or move on to another one? Why or why not?

   APPLY: (question 10, Day 5) Reflecting over the past three weeks' discussion of submission, what reasons for submitting struck you as the most compelling? How will you change your approach to a key relationship because of what you have learned?

WRAP-UP: What impacted you most within this week's passage of 1 Peter? How has Peter challenged your view of what submission looks like? What are the words of Peter asking of you personally?

VIDEO

Now watch the teaching video with your group. After the video concludes, close in prayer. Shape your praise, thanks, confession, and requests around what the Lord has been showing you from 1 Peter this week.

NOTES

WEEK 8:

SELF-CONTROLLED & SOBER-MINDED
1 PETER 4

We ended last week with the assurance that Jesus was seated at the right hand of God, victorious over suffering and death. Having exhorted us to endure mistreatment with grace by remembering Christ's work, Peter now moves from endurance to action. How should the believer regard sin? What behaviors should be avoided? What behaviors should be embraced? How should we steward the gifts we have been given? And how can we learn not just to endure suffering, but to find joy in it?

Though written two thousand years ago, Peter's practical encouragement is timeless, applicable to believers of all ages and stations, across all generations. Prepare to see yourself in the text this week. Ask God to help you learn right thinking, right expectation, and right reverence from Peter's faithful message.

DAY ONE

READ 1 PETER FROM BEGINNING TO END.

1. Spend some time committing to memory the verses you chose to learn.

2. Now look back at this week's section of text: 4:1-19. What does this passage teach us about God?

3. What do you think Peter wants to communicate in 4:1-19? Boil down his point to three or four bullet points.

4. How does this section flow logically out of the previous one? Specifically, what is the word *therefore* pointing back to in chapter 3?

DAY TWO

LOOK AT 4:1-6.

1. With an orange pencil, draw a box around every occurrence of the phrase *in the flesh* in 4:1-6. What do you think Peter means when he uses this phrase?

2. What do you think is meant by "Christ suffered in the flesh" (4:1)? Look back at 3:18 to help you with your answer. (Hint: It refers here to a specific event.)

3. What do you think Peter means by "whoever has suffered in the flesh has ceased from sin" (4:1)?

4. Have you ever suffered in a way that caused you to cease from sin? What did you endure and how did it change you?

5. Peter tells us to adopt the same way of thinking that Christ had with regard to sin. What exact wording does he use in 4:1?

   ☐ clothe yourselves

   ☐ wash yourselves

   ☐ arm yourselves

   What does his word choice imply about dealing with sin? How does 2:11 support your answer?

Look up 2 Corinthians 10:3-5. Note how it reinforces your answer above.

6. Look back through chapters 1–3 and note what "way(s) of thinking" (NIV: *attitudes*) of Christ's that Peter has already shown us to imitate.

Of the attitudes you wrote down, which one is hardest for you to "arm yourself" with? Why?

7. To whom is Peter referring when he uses the term *Gentiles*? Read 4:3 in the NIV to help with your answer. What term might modern-day Christians use?

8. Read through the list of sinful behaviors that characterized the unbelievers of Peter's time. If any of the terms are unclear to you, look them up in a dictionary. Does this list seem outdated or extreme? Why or why not?

9. Does this list of sinful behaviors seem exhaustive? Does Peter intend to communicate every type of sin we should avoid?

Read Ephesians 5:1-21. In the chart below, note every way that Paul reinforces or expands on Peter's exhortation in 4:3.

1 Peter 4:3, Peter said:	Ephesians 5:1-21, Paul said:
For the time that is past suffices for doing what the Gentiles want to do …	
… living in sensuality, passions, drunkenness, orgies, drinking parties, and lawless idolatry	

10. What sinful behavior do you need to cease that you have given "sufficient time" to in the past? Look up Ephesians 6:10-18. Spend some time in prayer, asking God to help you arm yourself against the particular sin He brought to mind.

DAY THREE

1. What two responses should we expect from unbelievers when we flee from sin (4:4)? List them below. Beside each, write why you think they respond that way.

2. How does what Peter says in 4:4-5 tie back to the idea in 2:23?

3. Now look at 4:6. We will talk about it in our teaching time, but for now, let's get some context for what Peter is saying.

Believers in Peter's time expected Christ's return to be very soon. When some began dying and the Lord had not yet returned, some believers faced a crisis of faith. Unbelievers mocked them for their belief in the resurrection, pointing to the deaths of their fellow believers as evidence that it was a vain hope.

Look up 1 Thessalonians 4:13-18. How did Paul speak to the dismay these believers were experiencing with regard to the death of their fellow believers and the return of Christ?

Now read 2 Peter 3:1-7. In his second letter to the churches in Asia minor, how did Peter address this same issue more fully?

In what way are all living people, saved and unsaved, "judged in the flesh" (4:6)? Look up Romans 5:12 to confirm your answer.

In light of what you learned above, how might you interpret Peter's words in 4:6?

4. How are Peter's words in 4:5-6 intended as an encouragement to believers to endure mocking from unbelievers?

5. Have you ever been mocked or ridiculed for your beliefs? How did you respond?

6. Rewrite 4:1-6 in your own words.

DAY FOUR

NOW LOOK AT 4:7-11.

1. In this section, Peter urges believers to embrace several different disciplines in light of the imminent return of Christ. What are they? What reason does he give for embracing them?

	Do this …	So that/because …
4:7		
4:8		
4:9		
4:10-11		

2. Which of the commands above does Peter indicate is most important? Why do you think this is so?

3. How might being self-controlled and sober-minded aid our prayers (4:7)?

4. What is the difference between showing hospitality and entertaining guests (4:9)? Why might showing hospitality make us want to grumble?

5. What does 4:10 reveal about the purpose of gifts from God? What do we sometimes wrongly believe to be the purpose of spiritual gifts? Why?

6. Peter mentions only a few specific spiritual gifts here. What other gifts do you know of? Look up Romans 12:6-8 and 1 Corinthians 12:8-10 to help with your answer. In addition to what you read there, can you think of other gifts not mentioned specifically by Peter or Paul?

7. What do you think might be your strongest spiritual gift from God?

How does the body of believers suffer if you use your gift for the wrong reasons?

How does the body of believers benefit if you use your gift for the right reasons?

8. Rewrite 4:7-11 in your own words.

DAY FIVE

NOW LOOK AT 4:12-19.

1. In 4:12-13, Peter gives two instructions regarding trials. What are they?

   4:12

   4:13

2. What does our surprise at fiery trials reveal about our expectations?

   Look up the following verses and note what each says about trials and expectations:

   John 15:18-21

   Philippians 1:29

3. Why does Peter say we should rejoice in persecution (4:13-14)?

   Read James 1:2-4 and note how James expands on Peter's words.

4. Peter says that "the Spirit of glory and of God rests upon [those insulted for the name of Christ]" (4:14). What do you think he means? Look up the following verses to help with your answer:
   Matthew 10:17-20

   John 14:16-18

   John 14:26

   Romans 8:26

   2 Corinthians 3:5-18

5. Look at 4:15. Peter gives examples of reasons we might suffer deservedly. Is there a sense in which this whole list could describe of any of us? Or does Peter mean it as an exaggerated list?

6. Why might we be ashamed to suffer for Christ (4:16)?

7. What is Peter's point in 4:17-19 regarding the judgment of the righteous and the unrighteous? Look up the following verses to help.
   Proverbs 11:31

   1 Corinthians 11:32

8. Keeping in mind that this is a letter of encouragement, how does Peter want us to be encouraged by contemplating the last judgment?

9. Is your first response to suffering to "commit yourself to your faithful Creator and continue to do good" (4:19)? What wrong thinking can cause us to have a different reaction?

10. Rewrite 4:12-19 in your own words.

WRAP-UP

What impacted you the most within this week's passage of 1 Peter? How has Peter challenged you to set aside sin and endure suffering? What are the words of Peter asking of you personally?

WEEK 8 GROUP DISCUSSION

INTRODUCTORY QUESTION: What is your favorite gift to receive, no matter how many times you receive it?

1. OBSERVE: (question 3, Day 2) What do you think Peter means by "whoever has suffered in the flesh has ceased from sin" (4:1)?

   APPLY: (question 4, Day 2) Have you ever suffered in a way that caused you to cease from sin? What did you endure and how did it change you?

2. OBSERVE: (question 1, Day 3) What two responses should we expect from unbelievers when we flee from sin (4:4)? Why?

   APPLY: (question 5, Day 3) Have you ever been mocked or ridiculed for your beliefs? How did you respond?

3. OBSERVE: (question 5, Day 4) What does 4:10 reveal about the purpose of gifts from God? What do we sometimes wrongly believe to be the purpose of spiritual gifts? Why?

   APPLY: (question 7, Day 4) What do you think might be your strongest spiritual gift from God? How does the body of believers suffer if you use your gift for the wrong reasons? How does the body of believers benefit if you use your gift for the right reasons?

4. OBSERVE: (question 4, Day 5) Peter says that "the Spirit of glory and of God rests upon [those insulted for the name of Christ]" (4:14). What do you think he means?

   APPLY: (question 9, Day 5) Is your first response to suffering to commit yourself to your faithful Creator and continue to do good (4:19)? What wrong thinking can cause us to have a different reaction?

WRAP-UP: What impacted you the most within this week's passage of 1 Peter? How has Peter challenged you to set aside sin and endure suffering? What are the words of Peter asking of you personally?

VIDEO

Now watch the teaching video with your group. After the video concludes, close in prayer. Shape your praise, thanks, confession, and requests around what the Lord has been showing you from 1 Peter this week.

NOTES

WEEK 9:

CLOTHED IN HUMILITY
1 PETER 5

As Peter winds down his letter to the church, he concludes with an exhortation to those charged with leading it. His message matters, not just for those in authority, but for those under it. We will work to hear chapter 5 as those who lead and as those who are led. Because all Scripture is God-breathed and profitable, we will even spend time looking at Peter's final greetings to see what treasure they hold.

As you read through the Book of 1 Peter for the last time (and hopefully the ninth time) during the study, pay attention to how your understanding has deepened since the first time you read it. How has the Lord used this brief letter to restore, confirm, strengthen, and establish you in your faith? Read with gratitude that the Word of God truly is living and active.

DAY ONE

READ 1 PETER FROM BEGINNING TO END.

1. Spend some time committing to memory the passage you chose.

2. Now look back at this week's section of text: 5:1-14. What does this passage teach us about God?

3. What do you think Peter wants to communicate in 5:1-14? Summarize his point in three or four bullet points.

4. How does this section flow logically out of the previous one?

DAY TWO

LOOK AT 5:1-4. READ IT IN THE ESV AND THE NIV.

1. How does Peter say he is qualified to appeal to church leaders (elders) (5:1)? Of all the qualifications he could have appealed to, why do you think he chooses these in particular?

2. What occupation is the position of elder compared to (5:2)? _____
Think about the role and tasks of a shepherd. What makes this a fitting analogy for a church leader? Think of at least three parallels.

3. What three wrong reasons for accepting a position in church leadership does Peter give (5:2-3)?
   1.

   2.

   3.

4. Why might a church leader feel he was serving under compulsion instead of willingly?

5. Why might a church leader serve for shameful gain?

6. Why might a church leader domineer instead of setting an example? Specifically, what kind of desirable example do you think is implied here?

7. What important reminder is given to leaders in 5:4?

8. How might the flock behave in such a way that the job of the shepherds is made easier? How might the flock help keep an elder from slipping into serving for the wrong reasons or out of the wrong attitude?

9. Do you think it would be difficult or easy to be a leader of a church body? Why or why not? How can you pray for your pastor, elders, and staff in this regard?

10. Rewrite 5:1-4 in your own words.

DAY THREE

NOW LOOK AT 5:5-7 IN THE ESV AND NIV.

1. What theme does Peter return to in these four verses?

2. How does 5:5 give a framework for all of us, whether in authority or subject to authority, to relate to one another?

3. Over whom do you have authority? How can you clothe yourself in humility toward that person?

4. Who has authority over you? How can you clothe yourself in humility toward that person?

5. What does Proverbs 3:34 promise the Lord will give to those who walk in humility?

6. Look up the following verses and note how each reinforces the importance of humility in the believer.

    Luke 6:41-42

    Luke 17:7-10

    Romans 12:3,16

    James 4:1-6

7. How does the message of 5:6-7 summarize Peter's thoughts on submission?

8. What anxieties do you feel when the topic of submitting to authority is raised (5:7)? How can you cast those anxieties on God?

9. Rewrite 5:5-7 in your own words.

DAY FOUR

NOW LOOK AT 5:8-11.

1. In 5:7, what did Peter tell us to take our minds off of? In 5:8, what does he tell us to devote our minds to?

2. What image does Peter use for our adversary, the Devil? How is this a fitting illustration? Think of at least three behavioral parallels.

3. How does Peter say we can resist the Devil in 5:8-9?

   Bearing in mind that Peter has been addressing the temptations we fall prey to when we suffer persecution, look at Ephesians 6:11-18 once again. How can the words of Paul help you in your efforts to resist the temptations suffering brings? Specifically, note how each item mentioned offers protection from Satan's attacks.

4. What does the God of all grace have in store for your future (5:10)? How does this thought encourage you to suffer well?

5. Do you think that 5:10 describes what God will do for us here (on earth) or hereafter (in heaven)? Explain your answer.

6. Why does Peter include 5:11 in his letter? What mechanical purpose does it serve? What spiritual purpose does it serve?

7. In chapters 2–5, Peter has moved back and forth between two topics: submission and responding to trials. How are these two ideas related?

8. Rewrite 5:8-11 in your own words.

DAY FIVE

NOW LOOK AT 5:12-14.

1. Who does Peter say he entrusted his letter to? _____.

   Look at the NIV to find the name by which he is more commonly known:

   _____

   Remember him? Look up the following verses to learn more about
   Peter's helper.
   Acts 15:22

   Acts 15:32

   Acts 15:40

   1 Thessalonians 1:1

   2 Thessalonians 1:1

2. Babylon (5:13) represented the height of godlessness and domination to
   the Old Testament prophets. What city might Peter be referencing here?
   [Hint: Where is Peter writing from?]

3. Who do you think "she who is at Babylon, who is likewise chosen" refers to? Look up 2 John 1 and 13 to help with your answer. [Hint: "She" is not a person, but a group of people, often referred to in the Bible in female terms.]

4. Who is "Mark, my son"? Choose the answer below that seems most likely.

☐ Mark is Peter's natural-born son.

☐ Mark is John Mark, mentioned throughout the Book of Acts as Peter's co-laborer and Paul's travel companion. He is also the author of one of the four Gospels.

5. I'm going to assume you got that last question correct. What can we learn about the early church from the way Peter speaks of Silvanus ("faithful brother"), Mark ("my son"), and his greeting of choice ("greet one another with the kiss of love")?

6. How good is the modern church at prioritizing and pursuing deep relationship with one another? What steps could we take to grow in this regard?

7. Rewrite 5:12-14 in your own words.

WRAP-UP

What impacted you the most within this week's passage of 1 Peter? How has Peter challenged you to view those in authority over you in the church? How has he encouraged you in the face of difficulties? What are the words of Peter asking of you personally?

WEEK 9 GROUP DISCUSSION

INTRODUCTORY QUESTION: What is the most unpleasant but necessary job or task you have ever had to perform?

1. **OBSERVE:** (question 2, Day 2) Think about the role and tasks of a
shepherd (5:2). What makes this a fitting analogy for a church leader?
Discuss at least three parallels.

   APPLY: (question 8, Day 2) How might the flock behave in such a way
   that the job of the shepherd is made easier? How might the flock help
   keep an elder from slipping into serving for the wrong reasons or out
   of the wrong attitude?

2. **OBSERVE:** (question 7, Day 3) How does the message of 5:6-7
summarize Peter's thoughts on submission?

   APPLY: (question 8, Day 3) What anxieties do you feel when the topic of
   submitting to authority is raised (5:7)? How can you cast those anxieties
   on God?

3. **OBSERVE:** (question 4, Day 4) What does the God of all grace have in
store for your future (5:10)? How does this thought encourage you to
suffer well?

   APPLY: (question 5, Day 4) Do you think that 5:10 describes what God
   will do for us here (on earth) or hereafter (in heaven)? Explain your
   answer.

4. **OBSERVE:** (question 5, Day 5) What can we learn about the early
church from the way Peter speaks of Silvanus ("faithful brother"),
Mark ("my son"), and his greeting of choice ("greet one another with
the kiss of love")?

   APPLY: (question 6, Day 5) How good is the modern church at
   prioritizing and pursuing deep relationship with one another? What
   steps could we take to grow in this regard?

WRAP-UP: What impacted you the most within this week's passage of 1
Peter? How has Peter challenged you to view those in authority over you in the
church? How has he encouraged you in the face of difficulties? What are the
words of Peter asking of you personally?

VIDEO

Now watch the teaching video with your group. After the video concludes, close in prayer. Shape your praise, thanks, confession, and requests around what the Lord has been showing you from 1 Peter this week.

NOTES

_____

_____

_____

_____

_____

_____

_____

_____

_____

_____

_____

_____

_____

_____

APPENDIX

FIRST PETER TEXT ENGLISH STANDARD VERSION

CHAPTER 1

GREETING

1 Peter, an apostle of Jesus Christ, To those who are elect exiles of the dispersion in Pontus, Galatia, Cappadocia, Asia, and Bithynia, 2 according to the foreknowledge of God the Father, in the sanctification of the Spirit, for obedience to Jesus Christ and for sprinkling with his blood:

May grace and peace be multiplied to you.

BORN AGAIN TO A LIVING HOPE

3 Blessed be the God and Father of our Lord Jesus Christ! According to his great mercy, he has caused us to be born again to a living hope through the resurrection of Jesus Christ from the dead, 4 to an inheritance that is imperishable, undefiled, and unfading, kept in heaven for you, 5 who by God's power are being guarded through faith for a salvation ready to be revealed in the last time. 6 In this you rejoice, though now for a little while, if necessary, you have been grieved by various trials, 7 so that the tested genuineness of your faith—more precious than gold that perishes though it is tested by fire—may be found to result in praise and glory and honor at the revelation of Jesus Christ. 8 Though you have not seen him, you love

him. Though you do not now see him, you believe in him and rejoice with joy that is inexpressible and filled with glory, 9 obtaining the outcome of your faith, the salvation of your souls.

10 Concerning this salvation, the prophets who prophesied about the grace that was to be yours searched and inquired carefully, 11 inquiring what person or time the Spirit of Christ in them was indicating when he predicted the sufferings of Christ and the subsequent glories. 12 It was revealed to them that they were serving not themselves but you, in the things that have now been announced to you through those who preached the good news to you by the Holy Spirit sent from heaven, things into which angels long to look.

CALLED TO BE HOLY

13 Therefore, preparing your minds for action, and being sober-minded, set your hope fully on the grace that will be brought to you at the revelation of Jesus Christ. 14 As obedient children, do not be conformed to the passions of your former ignorance, 15 but as he who called you is holy, you also be holy in all your conduct, 16 since it is written, "You shall be holy, for I am holy." 17 And if you call on him as Father who judges impartially according to each one's deeds, conduct yourselves with fear throughout the time of your exile, 18 knowing that you were ransomed from the futile ways inherited from your forefathers, not with perishable things such as silver or gold, 19 but with the precious blood of Christ, like that of a lamb without blemish or spot. 20 He was foreknown before the foundation of the world but was made manifest in the last times for the sake of you

21 who through him are believers in God, who raised him from the dead and gave him glory, so that your faith and hope are in God.

22 Having purified your souls by your obedience to the truth for a sincere brotherly love, love one another earnestly from a pure heart, 23 since you have been born again, not of perishable seed but of imperishable, through the living and abiding word of God; 24 for

"All flesh is like grass

and all its glory like the flower of grass.

The grass withers,

and the flower falls,

25 but the word of the Lord remains forever."

And this word is the good news that was preached to you.

CHAPTER 2

A LIVING STONE AND A HOLY PEOPLE

1 So put away all malice and all deceit and hypocrisy and envy and all slander. 2 Like newborn infants, long for the pure spiritual milk, that by it you may grow up into salvation— 3 if indeed you have tasted that the Lord is good.

4 As you come to him, a living stone rejected by men but in the sight of God chosen and precious, 5 you yourselves like living stones are being built up as a spiritual house, to be a holy priesthood, to offer spiritual sacrifices acceptable to God through Jesus Christ. 6 For it stands in Scripture:

"Behold, I am laying in Zion a stone,

a cornerstone chosen and precious,

and whoever believes in him will not be put to shame."

7 So the honor is for you who believe, but for those who do not believe,

"The stone that the builders rejected

has become the cornerstone,"

8 and

"A stone of stumbling,

and a rock of offense."

They stumble because they disobey the word, as they were destined to do.

9 But you are a chosen race, a royal priesthood, a holy nation, a people for his own possession, that you may proclaim the excellencies of him who called you out of darkness into his marvelous light. 10 Once you were not a people, but now you are God's people; once you had not received mercy, but now you have received mercy.

11 Beloved, I urge you as sojourners and exiles to abstain from the passions of the flesh, which wage war against your soul. 12 Keep your conduct among the Gentiles honorable, so that when they speak against you as evildoers, they may see your good deeds and glorify God on the day of visitation.

SUBMISSION TO AUTHORITY

13 Be subject for the Lord's sake to every human institution, whether it be to the emperor as supreme, 14 or to governors as sent by him to punish those who do evil and to praise those who do good. 15 For this is the will of God, that by doing good you should put to silence the ignorance of foolish people. 16 Live as people who are free, not using your freedom as a cover-up for evil, but living as servants of God. 17 Honor everyone. Love the brotherhood. Fear God. Honor the emperor.

18 Servants, be subject to your masters with all respect, not only to the good and gentle but also to the unjust. 19 For this is a gracious thing, when, mindful of God, one endures sorrows while suffering unjustly. 20 For what credit is it if, when you sin and are beaten for it, you endure? But if when you do good and suffer for it you endure, this is a gracious thing in the sight of God. 21 For to this you have been called, because Christ also suffered for you, leaving you an example, so that you might follow in his steps. 22 He committed no sin, neither was deceit found in his mouth. 23 When he was reviled, he did not revile in return; when he suffered, he did not threaten, but continued entrusting himself to him who judges justly. 24 He himself bore our sins in his body on the tree, that we might die to sin and live to righteousness. By his wounds you have been healed. 25 For you were straying like sheep, but have now returned to the Shepherd and Overseer of your souls.

...fied through Jesus Christ. To him belong glory and dominion forever ... ever. Amen.

SUFFERING AS A CHRISTIAN

...2 Beloved, do not be surprised at the fiery trial when it comes upon you ...o test you, as though something strange were happening to you. 13 But ...rejoice insofar as you share Christ's sufferings, that you may also rejoice and be glad when his glory is revealed. 14 If you are insulted for the name of Christ, you are blessed, because the Spirit of glory and of God rests upon you. 15 But let none of you suffer as a murderer or a thief or an evildoer or as a meddler. 16 Yet if anyone suffers as a Christian, let him not be ashamed, but let him glorify God in that name. 17 For it is time for judgment to begin at the household of God; and if it begins with us, what will be the outcome for those who do not obey the gospel of God? 18 And

"If the righteous is scarcely saved,
what will become of the ungodly and the sinner?"

19 Therefore let those who suffer according to God's will entrust their souls to a faithful Creator while doing good.

CHAPTER 5

SHEPHERD THE FLOCK OF GOD

1 So I exhort the elders among you, as a fellow elder and a witness of the sufferings of Christ, as well as a partaker in the glory that is going to be revealed: 2 shepherd the flock of God that is among you, exercising

CHAPTER 3

WIVES AND HUSBANDS

1 Likewise, wives, be subject to your own husbands, so that even if some do not obey the word, they may be won without a word by the conduct of their wives, 2 when they see your respectful and pure conduct. 3 Do not let your adorning be external—the braiding of hair and the putting on of gold jewelry, or the clothing you wear— 4 but let your adorning be the hidden person of the heart with the imperishable beauty of a gentle and quiet spirit, which in God's sight is very precious. 5 For this is how the holy women who hoped in God used to adorn themselves, by submitting to their own husbands, 6 as Sarah obeyed Abraham, calling him lord. And you are her children, if you do good and do not fear anything that is frightening.

7 Likewise, husbands, live with your wives in an understanding way, showing honor to the woman as the weaker vessel, since they are heirs with you of the grace of life, so that your prayers may not be hindered.

SUFFERING FOR RIGHTEOUSNESS' SAKE

8 Finally, all of you, have unity of mind, sympathy, brotherly love, a tender heart, and a humble mind. 9 Do not repay evil for evil or reviling for reviling, but on the contrary, bless, for to this you were called, that you may obtain a blessing. 10 For

"Whoever desires to love life
and see good days,
let him keep his tongue from evil

and his lips from speaking deceit;

11 let him turn away from evil and do good;

let him seek peace and pursue it.

12 For the eyes of the Lord are on the righteous,

and his ears are open to their prayer.

But the face of the Lord is against those who do evil."

13 Now who is there to harm you if you are zealous for what is good? 14 But even if you should suffer for righteousness' sake, you will be blessed. Have no fear of them, nor be troubled, 15 but in your hearts honor Christ the Lord as holy, always being prepared to make a defense to anyone who asks you for a reason for the hope that is in you; yet do it with gentleness and respect, 16 having a good conscience, so that, when you are slandered, those who revile your good behavior in Christ may be put to shame. 17 For it is better to suffer for doing good, if that should be God's will, than for doing evil.

18 For Christ also suffered once for sins, the righteous for the unrighteous, that he might bring us to God, being put to death in the flesh but made alive in the spirit, 19 in which he went and proclaimed to the spirits in prison, 20 because they formerly did not obey, when God's patience waited in the days of Noah, while the ark was being prepared, in which a few, that is, eight persons, were brought safely through water. 21 Baptism, which corresponds to this, now saves you, not as a removal of dirt from the body but as an appeal to God for a good conscience, through the resurrection of Jesus Christ, 22 who has gone into heaven

and is at the right hand of God, with angels, a[...] having been subjected to him.

CHAPTER 4
STEWARDS OF GOD'S GRACE

1 Since therefore Christ suffered in the flesh, arm your[...] same way of thinking, for whoever has suffered in the fle[...] from sin, 2 so as to live for the rest of the time in the flesh[...] for human passions but for the will of God. 3 For the time th[...] suffices for doing what the Gentiles want to do, living in sensu[...] passions, drunkenness, orgies, drinking parties, and lawless ido[...] 4 With respect to this they are surprised when you do not join the[...] the same flood of debauchery, and they malign you; 5 but they will[...] account to him who is ready to judge the living and the dead. 6 For t[...] is why the gospel was preached even to those who are dead, that thoug[...] judged in the flesh the way people are, they might live in the spirit the[...] way God does.

7 The end of all things is at hand; therefore be self-controlled and sober-minded for the sake of your prayers. 8 Above all, keep loving one another earnestly, since love covers a multitude of sins. 9 Show hospitality to one another without grumbling. 10 As each has received a gift, use it to serve one another, as good stewards of God's varied grace: 11 whoever speaks, as one who speaks oracles of God; whoever serves, as one who serves by the strength that God supplies—in order that in everything God may be

oversight, not under compulsion, but willingly, as God would have you; not for shameful gain, but eagerly; 3 not domineering over those in your charge, but being examples to the flock. 4 And when the chief Shepherd appears, you will receive the unfading crown of glory. 5 Likewise, you who are younger, be subject to the elders. Clothe yourselves, all of you, with humility toward one another, for "God opposes the proud but gives grace to the humble."

6 Humble yourselves, therefore, under the mighty hand of God so that at the proper time he may exalt you, 7 casting all your anxieties on him, because he cares for you. 8 Be sober-minded; be watchful. Your adversary the devil prowls around like a roaring lion, seeking someone to devour. 9 Resist him, firm in your faith, knowing that the same kinds of suffering are being experienced by your brotherhood throughout the world. 10 And after you have suffered a little while, the God of all grace, who has called you to his eternal glory in Christ, will himself restore, confirm, strengthen, and establish you. 11 To him be the dominion forever and ever. Amen.

FINAL GREETINGS

12 By Silvanus, a faithful brother as I regard him, I have written briefly to you, exhorting and declaring that this is the true grace of God. Stand firm in it. 13 She who is at Babylon, who is likewise chosen, sends you greetings, and so does Mark, my son. 14 Greet one another with the kiss of love.

Peace to all of you who are in Christ.

NOTES

NOTES

Jen Wilkin

Jen Wilkin is a speaker, writer, and teacher of women's Bible studies in Dallas, TX. Her passion is to see women become articulate and committed followers of Christ, with a clear understanding of why they believe what they believe, grounded in the Word of God. She is the author of Women of the Word: How to Study the Bible with Both our Hearts and our Minds. *Her family calls The Village Church home.*

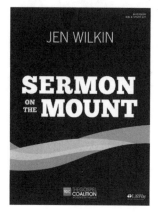

SERMON ON THE MOUNT
9 sessions

What does it mean to be a citizen of the kingdom of Heaven? *Sermon on the Mount* articulates what the life of a Christ-follower should look like, asking us the same questions it posed to its original hearers: How should a disciple relate to sin? To others? To the Law? How does a disciple think, speak, and act? Examine the words of Jesus in-depth as He challenges us to think differently about repentance, salvation, and sanctification.

Bible Study Book	005644876	**$12.99**
Leader Kit	005644877	**$59.99**

Contains DVDs & Bible Study Book with leader helps

Kathleen Nielson

Kathleen Nielson serves as director of women's initiatives for The Gospel Coalition. She holds M.A. and Ph.D. degrees in literature from Vanderbilt University and a B.A. from Wheaton College. Author of the Living Word Bible studies, she speaks often at women's conferences and loves working with women in studying the Bible. She shares a heart for students with her husband, Niel, president of Covenant College from 2002 to 2012 and now leading an enterprise developing resources for Christian schools around the world.

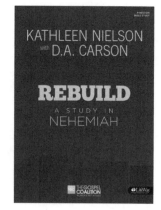

REBUILD: A STUDY IN NEHEMIAH
8 sessions

Delve into one of the most compelling Old Testament narratives—the story of Nehemiah leading God's people to rebuild Jerusalem's walls after the exile. Eight sessions set the story in its historical context while illuminating the larger biblical picture of God's redemptive plan. A courageous, prayerful leader, Nehemiah points us to God's sovereign plan to work through His people according to His promises and for His redemptive purposes in Jesus Christ. This study leads us to peer into the dramatic story of God's people sustained by God's Word at a crucial point in salvation history.

Bible Study Book	005644872	**$12.99**
Leader Kit	005644873	**$59.99**

Contains DVDs & Bible Study Book with leader helps

lifeway.com/gospelcoalition
800.458.2772 | LifeWay Christian Stores

Pricing and availability subject to change without notice.

LifeWay | Women